Trai
Vata

Brick By Brick

Building a Solid Foundation for Your Marriage

by Steven & Melisa Zimmerman

We want to hear from you. Please send any comments you have about this book to contact@bridgebuildermm.org

Brick by Brick: Building a Solid Foundation for Your Marriage

BRIDGE
BUILDER

This book is dedicated to:
John and Eileen Zimmerman
and Gene and June Marrow
Who loved until "Death did they part."

TABLE OF CONTENTS

FORWARD

Dream with me. Imagine your marriage thirty years from now. You discovered the secrets to a great marriage. You overcame life challenges. Your children married successfully. You are still fulfilling your purpose together with your spouse. How many children and grandchildren are surrounding you? What is your nickname? (Papa? Gramps? G-G? Meema?) What is your daily routine? How big is the smile on your face? Did you adopt children? Where do you live? Is your hair turning silver? What purpose are you fulfilling? How are you touching lives?

Don't be afraid to dream. This is a secret God gave to Abraham. God's promise to him called for acts of faith. Abraham was told to count the stars. I can see him standing outside late at night after the whole camp has gone to sleep. The night sky is lit up with stars and the evening breeze is perfect. There stands Abraham on a distant hill – the silhouette of a dreamer against a backdrop of innumerable stars. He is counting. He is dreaming of this family God has promised him. He sees a multitude that is without number. It is a family destined to bless nations.

We see Abraham's dream fulfilled. We consider his dream a basic fact of history. What about yours? Dream again.

If I asked you to picture your dream home, would you be more concerned about the quality of the foundation or the cost of the home? Most likely your concern is the cost. Mine too. The foundation is not even a thought, because laying a proper foundation is common knowledge for home builders.

However, laying a proper foundation for a great marriage is not common knowledge. Assumptions are often made where there should have been communication. These gaps become unfulfilled expectations and a foundation for future frustration and division. With God's wisdom, you can change this negative scenario.

The foundation of your marriage is the key to fulfilling God's purpose in your life. You can know the key areas for laying an excellent foundation, because they are presented in this book.

Steve and Melisa have laid it out in simple terms. They have prepared *Brick by Brick* as an excellent tool for couples, counselors, marriage ministry leaders, and pastors. You can't miss the details with this straightforward and instructional manual.

I encourage you to cover every topic with your spouse. I thoroughly enjoyed reading this book because you never get lost in a maze of statistics and stories. The facts are clear and the follow-through is simple.

Are you concerned about your children's marriage? Are you thinking of a great gift for a newlywed or an engaged couple? Send this book.

If you don't do well studying alone, find some friends and do a book study together. If you counsel couples, you have found a great tool. Whether you study this alone, in a community, or with a counselor, this resource will strengthen your foundation and prepare you for future success.

Before I married, I read books like these. This one is great!

You are not called to be a statistic. You are called to win. Dream again and let a solid foundation be your secret to success.

Clarence Hill Jr., Executive Director, Eye to Eye
and Celebrate Marriage Oklahoma

PREFACE

In a time when the market is saturated with self-help books, how do you determine which book is going to be right for you? Clearly, not everything out there is working. If it were, we wouldn't be in a society where over fifty percent of all marriages end in divorce. God has laid out a successful blueprint for successful marriages. Christ and the church lived that out, which is why our first and foremost source of information is the Bible. Many people would argue that learning from a book written over 2000 years ago isn't relevant to society today. My spouse and I share life lessons learned right here in the 21st century from our own marriage that has survived death, drugs, and division. We have come out on the other side stronger and more committed than before. We are called to share what we learned from those experiences with you. We also share lessons learned from real marriages that are experiencing success. Real success is not to be confused in any way, shape, or form with perfection, but the concept of a strong and successful marriage doesn't need to become extinct. We believe there can be a reverse in the current statistics and it starts by getting the big things right and dealing with serious issues before you ever say, "I do." When problems come up, and believe us, they will, you will be armed with the tools and techniques you need to successfully deal with them. Instead of a marriage being shaken to the core by a problem that seems too big, you wind up with a relationship that is stronger because of a God that is big enough for anything you will encounter.

This book offers information with practical applications. It provides relevant questions that stir conversations about hot button topics that can turn into marriage-threatening issues. If you are aware of the traps before you get to them, and have already developed plans to handle them, you increase your likelihood for successfully navigating those traps.

Communication is vital to any healthy marriage. As you answer the questions in each chapter, you develop lines of communication that, if maintained, will be the life-source of a healthy and successful marriage.

This book is designed to help you lay a stronger foundation for your marriage and establish an initial foundation of a God-centered marriage. Add to that foundation topics of his and her needs, conflict resolution, sex and intimacy, money, kids and family, and affair-proofing your marriage, then brick by brick you will build a foundation for a marriage that will last a lifetime.

A GOD-CENTERED MARRIAGE

A God-centered marriage is not possible unless both the husband and the wife have committed their own lives individually to serving God and doing whatever He calls them to do. It may seem that it goes without stating, but we feel like we have to state the obvious. Without this basic beginning point, it is not possible to have a God-centered life or a God-centered marriage. Once you have settled this point, then having a God-centered marriage becomes completely doable.

What does a God-centered marriage mean? What does a God-centered marriage look like? These questions can be answered by looking at why God created marriage. In Genesis 2:24 we see that God created marriage to be between one man and one woman. *"That is why a man leaves his father and mother and is united to his wife, and they become one flesh."* Two reasons that God created marriage were for companionship and also to serve as a picture of what the relationship between Christ and the church would look like.

Ephesians 5:22 tells us that everything we do in our marriage should be done as unto the Lord. Therefore, in order to have a God- centered marriage, we choose to love our spouse according to the plan laid out for us in the Bible as an act of worship and obedience to God.

When this serves as the primary focus in marriage, it allows God to bless the marriage. By making your marriage an act of obedience and worship, it switches your focus from what your spouse is doing for you, to what you are doing for God.

When my spouse and I met, we lived several states apart. We spent hours on the telephone every day. This primarily would not start until after 9pm. Some nights when we did our daily Bible study and prayer, our prayer would be interrupted by someone snoring, not that the prayers weren't heartfelt and passionate, it was just really late.

Had we been focused on each other, we could have been offended, but we were focused on God. We still laugh about it to this day. That is one example of what a God-centered marriage looks like.

God-centered marriage will always have the stated

goal that we will not make any decisions apart from the Word of God and leading of the Holy Spirit. This means that all major relationship decisions will be driven specifically by what the Word of God says or by Biblical principles.

However, minor decisions such as coffee, tea, or soda can be made independently. Jesus told his disciples, *"I only speak what the Father says to me"* (John 12:50). It was this one singular act of devotion to God's word by Jesus that enabled Him to live a perfect life and fulfill His divine purpose on Calvary.

If we embrace this philosophy, then our lives will be free of a lot of unnecessary frustration. All too often, we chose to speak and act in ways that are driven by our hurt, emotions, or desires rather than speaking and acting in a way that brings God glory. This one simple principle, when applied to every decision, every word, and every action, will change your lives and your relationship forever.

With these principles in mind, take some time and see where they fit into your life. Answer the following questions on an individual basis and then discuss them with each other.

Where does God stand in your life at this time?

I feel that I'm pretty good
at trusting God with larger
issues, though I struggle
trusting Him with smaller
issues.

What does a God-Centered Marriage look like to you?

It is a relationship in which both people love God so wholly that it becomes easy to show love to the other person even when they may not do the same.

Every child is born a blank slate both about God and about marriage. What we learn, we learn from the people around us. What we learn about marriage is what we see modeled by our family. In most cases, we become a wife or husband very similar to our parents, or if that was something very negative, we will likely become the opposite of what we saw in our parents. Because of this, we have to be very deliberate in our efforts to become what the Bible says we should be as husbands and wives.

If you came from a Godly home where your parents demonstrated a Godly marriage, this will be much easier. If you didn't, then it will take much more effort and study to develop the marriage prescribed by the Bible.

This effort will be rewarded with a higher likelihood of success. Take some time and think about what you learned from your family about marriage.

Answer the following question separately and then discuss your answers.

What did you learn from your parents about a God-Centered Marriage?

That no matter how big a disagreement may seem God can take it and use it to make something great come from it

Daily Bible Study

Daily Bible study can build the foundation necessary for a successful marriage and is an essential part of any God-centered marriage.

This should be done both individually and as a couple every day. When you spend time daily in the Word of God , you open up the opportunity for God to speak to you through His word. Just as food is essential for our physical body to maintain health, daily Bible study is vital for our spiritual health. When couples spend time in Bible study together, their spiritual health improves.

This doesn't have to be something that is long and exhaustive every day. Sometimes a simple study using a devotional or a few Bible verses can be very impactful. One day we had a very busy day going from work to watch a double-header baseball game played by our boys. We realized on the way that we had not done our Bible study for that day and didn't have a Bible in the car with us. Back in the day, our phones were barely literate and could by no stretch be called "smart phones," so we couldn't access the Bible on our phones. After choosing the always popular memory verse, John 11:35 *"Jesus wept"* we spent the next 30 minutes talking about Jesus' humanity and compassion. God will always honor your time and dedication to Him by showing up.

Take some time and answer the following questions independently and then working together identify ways you will implement daily Bible Study.

In what ways are you currently participating in personal Bible study?

Currently I do not participate in a personal devotion, I frequently let life get in the way.

What tools will you use to ensure daily Bible study as a couple?

We are currently working through "Hand in hand" and would like to start "Crazy Love".

Prayer

Prayer is the direct communication with God. It is a very powerful tool in a personal relationship with God. Ephesians 6:18 states that prayer is a part of the "Armor of God."

As a couple, there is nothing more powerful than the prayer of agreement. With the man in place as the spiritual leader of the home, his prayer over his wife will help ensure that unity is maintained.

When couples make a priority of their prayer time together, a bond is formed between them and God that makes His amazing power available to them. In Matthew 18:19 the Bible says, *"when two or more shall agree concerning anything you ask in prayer, it will be done for you."*

It is very difficult to be in conflict with someone that you are praying for and/or praying with. Starting and ending the day praying together is a vital part of a healthy relationship.

What will you do together to ensure that daily prayer becomes a priority?

We have started praying for blessing on each other every night before bed and will continue to do so for the rest of our lives as we both recognize the importance of joint prayer

The Three Strand Cord

Ecclesiastes 4:12 says, *"Though one may be overpowered, two can defend themselves. A cord of three strands is not easily broken."* This passage of scripture illustrates the importance of the covenant relationship between a husband and wife intertwined with God. This causes the strands to become one cord, which is not only difficult to break, but is very difficult to separate. This symbol of a God-centered marriage serves as a reminder that His love will continue to bind you together as one for the entirety of your marriage.

Another great reminder we receive from the three strand cord is if one of the cords becomes stressed or frayed, the other strands will ensure that the cord remains intact giving the stressed or frayed cord time to heal. Even in those times in a marriage when both partners are stressed or at their breaking point, God will hold the marriage together as each person works to regain wholeness. God is not a strand that can be broken and He is able to hold the cord together as long as the other cords do not separate themselves from Him.

In our second year of marriage, I (Melisa) had just lost my mom after a lengthy battle with breast cancer. I was very close to my mother. In fact, we had been living with her and my dad for several weeks prior to her death.

This brought me to one of the lowest times in my life. I was depressed and even angry with God for not healing my mom. For many weeks following my mom's death, I was not only disengaged from life, I was mostly disengaged from my marriage. In the place of brokenness it would have been easy for Steven to become frustrated and upset with me. However, his dedication and focus on God kept him in a place where he was able to provide the support I needed to heal. This is our favorite picture of the "3-strand cord" in our marriage.

There have been other times when Steven was in a low place or struggling with an issue in life and I was able to support and encourage him by remaining in a place of focus on God for our marriage. Even if you find that both of you are in a low place at the same time, that is the place where you will see God holding both of you together as you continue to maintain your relationship with Him.

One of our favorite scriptures is 2 Corinthians 12:9. Paul tells the people at Corinth that in his times of weakness God's power is made perfect. We can have this confidence that even when both spirits are lagging, God will hold us together.

With these ideas in mind, work together to answer the following question.

What are some ways you can identify that indicate your commitment to the three-strand cord?

I do my best to love her according to Gods word and I'm willing to admit when I'm wrong. When she comes to me with a concern I try to pray with her and help her give it to God

Team Names

What is a team name and why do we need one? This is a name that you choose together for you and your spouse or future spouse. It simply helps us remember an important key– we are on the same team. We're teammates, not opponents and when things start to feel like we're opponents, we can recognize this as an attempt of Satan to cause division. The Enemy loves division. If he can get us to take each other down – oh how easy his job becomes! If he can get us to be destructive towards each other, nit-pick, say critical and inaccurate things about each other's motives, have a negative or hurtful perception of the other, if he can get us to help him with his job, then he has gained a foothold in our lives. If he can get us to act more like we're on his team than our spouse's team – yikes!

The Bible says this truth:

For our struggle is not against flesh and blood, but against the rulers, against the authorities, against the powers of this dark world and against the spiritual forces of evil in the heavenly realms. - Ephesians 6:12

Our enemy is not our spouse. Our enemy is sin and Satan. There is such strength in a united husband, wife, and the Lord! Those three strands united as a team create an alliance, solidarity, and strength unmatched by anything else!

So we commit to:

Be alert and of sober mind. Your enemy the devil prowls around like a roaring lion looking for someone to devour. - 1 Peter 5:8

By choosing to stay alert, we commit to team unity and achieving goals to help us move through every situation with unity and strength. With courage and fortitude, we defeat inklings of accusation or blame, and we keep the devil from gaining a foothold in our lives!

Therefore what God has joined together, let no one separate. - Mark 10:9

Amen!! In the strength and solidarity of the Lord, commitment to a team mindset enables wonderful victory!

Every couple, even those who have been together for even a short period of time have some sort of inside joke and that shared story often provides a perfect opportunity to give birth to your team name. The best team names are going to evoke warm memories and smiles every time they are mentioned and will serve as a warm reminder of why you got married in the first place. It will also remind you of the value of your marriage to each other and to God.

Because we are sure you're asking, "So, Mr. & Mrs. Perfect, what's your team name?" Our team name is the awe inspiring, "Cake Toppers." We know that you are on the edge of your seat with anticipation wondering just how we could come up with such an inspirational team name.

Here's the story: God planted in us a dream of marriage ministry early on in our relationship. We dreamed about it, prayed about it and pursued what we believed God was calling us to do. However, given my (Melisa's) unsuccessful 20-year marriage this seemed sort of a stretch for us. As we continued to follow the dream, God began to reveal the concept of the wedding cake and how it could be used to teach about marriage and rela-tionship. The two things that most people remember about a wedding are the dress and the cake.

At the top of the cake is where the bride and groom stand. The cake-topper symbolizes the bride and the groom at their closest together. Because being in unity is so vital to a marriage, we chose the name "Cake Toppers." This silly name is used frequently to bring a smile to the other person or encouragement in a tough time or just as conversation point to teach others about marriage. There you go! The abridged version of how we became this team. "Go Cake-Toppers!!" With this idea in mind, work together to find your great team name.

What is your team Name?

Frequent Flyers

Briefly describe why you chose your team name and what the meaning behind it is:

Chose it because we have to fly back and forth to see each other.

WE ALL HAVE NEEDS!
HIS NEEDS

Having a loving and satisfying marriage is one of the best blessings we can have. There is nothing more peaceful and powerful than a husband and wife who love each other and meet each others needs. When you understand the needs of your spouse, you are then able to identify ways to meet his/her needs. This is a recipe for a successful marriage.

When needs in a marriage go unmet, the likelihood of an affair increases. Statistics say that half of all marriages will experience infidelity. In spite of these stats, we must say that there is never any excuse for an affair. It is important to remember that Satan operates in unmet needs. The devil hates marriage because it is so sacred to God. Most people take the energy that God gave them to love each other and use it to try and change the other person. When you reject your spouse's needs, you reject your spouse. You are different by God's design.

Men and women have basic needs. These needs are generally true of most men and women. There is no way to speak to all the shades of grey in the needs area. In this book we will speak in generalities.

While needs are vital, it is important that we view them through the proper lens. We don't view needs through a lens of selfishness in relationship to ourselves. We view them outwardly to meeting the needs of our spouse. Jesus said himself, *"I came not to be served but to serve."* Matthew 20:28

We have often found that when teaching about the needs of a man and a woman, this knowledge is used as the measuring stick for whether or not someone's spouse is meeting their needs. This is completely backwards from the way this insight should be used. The insight must ONLY be used as knowledge you have to make sure that YOU are meeting the needs of your spouse. By looking at this information from the wrong vantage point you are setting yourself up for significant problems.

It is important to identify the needs of each person. We will start with the four basic needs of men. These needs are respect, sex, fellowship and domestic support. All of these needs are vital, and when a wife is meeting all the needs of her spouse, she is not only ensuring a good relationship, but she is following the pattern set out in the Bible.

The first and primary need of a man is respect. Ephesians 5:33 says *"But this also applies to you; every husband must love his wife as himself and every wife must respect her husband."* (emphasis added)

Respect looks different for men than it does for women. When women disrespect men, it is especially hurtful. It is undermining, and leads to an emotional distance that creates long-term problems.

What men view as disrespect is usually something that women do not. For example, telling a joke to your friends where your husband is the object of ridicule, or something he did that provides the humor for the joke is very disrespectful to men. Women often just see it as something funny.

Correcting your spouse in front of others is very disrespectful as well, while most women just see it as being helpful. Criticizing his work performance or ability to generate income is also another area where women can be perceived as very disrespectful. These are just a few ways that men and women view disrespect differently. A heightened awareness of disrespectful behavior is going to prevent you from unintentionally hurting your husband and damaging your relationship.

One of the best ways to identify disrespect is to ask your husband directly: "What do I do that comes across as disrespectful to you?" Word of warning, if you are not diligently looking at this as a way to gain insight about how to make your relationship better, you can easily find yourself with your feelings hurt and feeling judged or condemned. Approaching this often difficult conversation in a loving way will help prevent unnecessary offense.

Having discussed what disrespect looks like, we need to take some time and talk about what respect looks like. There are many ways to demonstrate respect, but nothing demonstrates respect more than a few simple words such as, "I trust your judgment," "I know you have the best interests of our family at heart," or "I'm behind you one hundred percent." By allowing your husband to be the head of the household as we are instructed in the Bible, you are clearly demonstrating your respect for him and his position.

For some women this is a difficult undertaking, especially if you have never seen this behavior modeled. By being diligent to study the Word and by reading books on the subject, you will be able to increase your knowledge and capacity to exhibit respect. If you feel that you don't have time to read books, there are many great blogs that you can read and follow to learn practical ways to demonstrate respect to your husband.

Women who learn how to be respectful wives are some of the smartest women in the world. They also tend to have some of the best marriages.

Take some time and answer the following questions and then get together and review your answers.

What are some practical ways that each of you feel demonstrates respect?

Him:

Listening to and considering my opinion. Not treating me like a child.

Her:

_____

_____

_____

_____

_____

_____

_____

Both: Discuss some changes that can be made to more effectively demonstrate respect.

_____

_____

_____

_____

_____

_____

_____

_____

_____

_____

_____

_____

Sex is the second most important need for men. The only thing that will likely surprise anyone about this section is that sex is not the most important need for men. It is, however, a very important need and must be seen as that. Sex in marriage is something designed by God, and is a part of a man's basic makeup. The scripture clearly indicates that both the husband and wife need to be involved. Sex is not a bartering tool, or a weapon, but it is designed to be an integral part of marriage. All too often we find that women tend to use withholding sex as a manipulation tool or a punishment. This practice clearly goes against what is set forth in the Bible.

3 The husband should fulfill his wife's sexual needs, and the wife should fulfill her husband's needs. 4 The wife gives authority over her body to her husband, and the husband gives authority over his body to his wife. 5 Do not deprive each other of sexual relations, unless you both agree to refrain from sexual intimacy for a limited time so you can give yourselves more completely to prayer. Afterward, you should come together again so that Satan won't be able to tempt you because of your lack of self-control. 1 Corinthians 7:3-5

Inside marriage, sex allows for freedom of expression, but as with any good relationship, there are boundaries that need to be decided on and respected. Sex should never be done in a way that causes one of the spouses to feel degraded or demoralized. It is a loving act and each spouse should treat the other with the utmost respect and honor. Because God designed sex, try praying before and/or after sex. This will not only make sex more intimate, but will also discourage one spouse from dishonoring the boundaries.

Each of you define sex and romance, describing how the two are different and how the two interact

Sex is the actual physical act while romance is the emotional feelings that go with it. Sex without romance is hollow and unsatisfying.

The third need of a man is fellowship. There is nothing better than being married to your best friend. He wants you to be interested in the things that he is interested in. The wife needs to be willing to do the things that he likes to do, even if that means you need to learn more about sports, fishing, or any other interests he has. This is part of sacrificial love. This creates an environment where you can just have fun together. Fun is one of the elements that keeps a marriage alive and growing and prevents it from eroding into a business relationship.

I (Steven) really enjoy NASCAR. However, Melisa is not all that interested in watching cars go in circles for several hours at a time. She has learned enough about NASCAR to speak with some intelligence about it. While she may never know much about drafting, manufacturers, or pit times, she can tell you that my favorite driver is Denny Hamlin and he drives the number 11 FedEx Toyota Camry and she doesn't always get hysterical if I wear my Denny Hamlin gear to church on race day.

Luckily for me, Melisa was raised in a family that enjoyed sports. She is fairly knowledgeable about football and can totally hold her own when it comes to calling strikes and balls as well as being able to identify the infield fly rule. She will probably never watch WWE or golf with me, but there are enough things that we can enjoy together, even if they are not her favorite things.

Be careful not to use this process to martyr yourself. Spending time doing what he enjoys does not give you license to grumble and complain about never getting to do what you want. The more that this is done out of love, the more you are going to find it returned on his behalf.

Ladies, name the top five interests and hobbies of your guy:

_____

_____

_____

_____

_____

_____

Guys, name the top five interests and hobbies you would enjoy sharing with your gal:

X- wing miniatures game

Hiking

Archery

Golf

woodworking

Nasa/space History/physics

Finally the fourth basic need of men is domestic support. Wives have the ability to create the environment in the home. Every man needs a comforting and welcoming environment to come home to. After being in the workplace all day, they need a place to come and feel like they are valuable and important.

Ladies, this is one area where you can really shine. Even if you work outside the home, it is still a great opportunity to serve your husband. It may take some effort on your part, especially if you weren't raised in this kind of environment. However, by creating a warm and welcoming home for your husband, you also create a place he wants to come home to.

That can look differently to different people. You know your husband better than anyone else. He may need some space when he comes home to unwind, or maybe he needs to be doted on and be the center of your universe for a while.

Whether he needs space or attention, almost every man loves to be greeted at the door with a warm hug and a serious kiss. Whatever creative way you find to welcome your husband home, always be willing to make his homecoming something that demonstrates your gratefulness that he is home and your desire to meet his needs.

Domestic support also includes such things as cooking meals, cleaning the house, and providing clean clothing for him to wear. While these seem like mundane chores, they all speak loudly about your desire to serve him. Little things, like asking what he would like for dinner or picking up after him from time to time, are thoughtful gestures that if done consistently and out of a heart to serve him and love will not go unnoticed. Proverbs 31 gives a great example of what a Godly wife looks like. It is a great passage of scripture to study and implement in your relationship with your husband. By serving him in this way, you are creating a place where not only will he want to come home to, he will feel very valued and honored, which is something that God asks wives to do in His word.

Women, as a wife, what can you do to provide that kind of environment?

_____

_____

_____

_____

_____

_____

_____

_____

_____

_____

Men, what would be special ways that your wife could help create a wonderful home environment that would make you valued and honored?

- Tidy but not sterile house
- Do laundary (I hate doing laundry)
- allow me to have some personal time for projects.
- Not be annoyed at a small mess I may make but just mention it once and let me take care of it.

WE ALL HAVE NEEDS!
HER NEEDS

Marriage between a man and a woman and God was God's plan from the beginning. This union is the exact replication of the trinity. God refers to Christians as the Bride of Christ throughout the New Testament. As men walk out the truths of the Word, they will find that they fulfill the needs of their wife. Ephesians 5:25-26 tells husbands to love their wives as Christ loves the church and gives Himself up for her.

Having looked at men's needs in the previous chapter, we now examine the needs of women. Men's needs and women's needs are very different. This is a plan specifically designed by God. When husbands are able to identify and meet the needs of their wives, they find that unity becomes not only something that is achievable, but very powerful as well.

Again, it is important to note the needs of women we will identify in this chapter are given in generalities. There is not enough space to identify all the variations of these needs.

The needs of a woman include security, affection, open communication and leadership. Again, this list of needs are not given to be used as a measuring stick by the wife to determine if her husband is meeting her needs, but rather by the husband to provide practical ways to meet the needs of his wife. It is import to keep the proper perspective when we identify and implement the needs of a woman.

The first and primary need of a woman is security. A woman's need for security shows itself in four areas: Emotional, spiritual, physical, and financial security. For a woman, emotional security is an issue of the heart. Spiritual security is a soul issue. Physical security involves touch. The basis for financial security is wrapped in provision. As these needs are met, areas of insecurities decrease tremendously, which allows her to fully enjoy marriage. A secure wife is then in a better place to meet the needs of her husband.

An example of meeting an emotional security need is allowing freedom of expression. A woman who can reveal her true feelings without a threat of punishment or reprisal is more emotionally secure. If she feels that every thing she says or responds to with her true emotions causes a disturbance in her husband she will have a tendency to feel insecure. It is important for a husband to remember that women are highly charged emotional beings and this is exactly how God created them to be. If you support your wife on an emotional level you will find that this can bring about a much more stable and secure relationship.

Because men and women view emotions differently, it is easy for a husband to feel that if his wife is being emotional she is not able to think clearly or develop effective plans. However, because of the way that women process through emotions the very opposite is often the case. Men need to be careful not to under-value emotions. Men often see emotions as a weakness and he needs to honor that as an intricate part of a woman's make up and to deny her emotions is to deny her the emotional security that she needs.

Additionally, if a husband is willing to share his own emotions in an honest and non-threatening manner with his wife it will strengthen her security as well as the bonds that hold them together.

Spiritual security comes when a husband is actively engaged in the spiritual climate of the marriage. By leading his wife in spiritual activities such as prayer, Bible study and church involvement, he is providing an atmosphere where his wife will not only feel secure but be able to grow in her own relationship with God. Confidence in knowing you are providing spiritual security will cause your wife to be more connected to you and to God.

Spiritual security cannot be achieved by a "flash in the pan" kind of relationship with God. In order to achieve true security the husband must maintain a very connected relationship with God. This is important because the husband is the spiritual head of the household. When he shows that he takes this responsibility seriously it provides an atmosphere that fosters a very connected relationship.

It seems elementary that the first stage of physical security is that there is no threat to the wife from her husband. Sadly, due to the high incidence of domestic abuse, we need to make this point that there will never be physical security if your wife feels that you will ever raise you hand against her. The next stage in physical security is knowing in every situation you will protect her at all costs from any outside threat. The feeling of physical protection brings calmness like no other. This can be done in even small gestures that show you are looking out for her.

For instance, Melisa never wants to sleep on the side of the bed that is nearest the door. Her thoughts are that if anyone comes into our bedroom she wants them to have to go through me (Steven) first. There was also a time when I was not as diligent about checking the garage door at night to make sure that it was locked. This caused some insecurity in Melisa related the safety of our vehicles, her, and our daughter. Because security is not a major issue, it didn't even get on my radar. As I became aware that it was an issue for her, it was an opportunity for me to step up and meet a need and give her value.

Finally, financial security is often looked at as being materialistic, but it is a very real need and is one that needs to be taken seriously.

1 Timothy 5:8 tells us, "But if anyone does not provide for his own, and especially for those of his household, he has denied the faith, and is worse than an unbeliever."

You don't have to be a millionaire to provide financial security. What needs to be communicated is you are doing everything possible to meet the financial needs of the household. This may mean that you are diligent with your budget, that you are working consistently, or that you are not frivolous with your spending. If you have been dealt a blow and lost your job, she needs to know that you are working tirelessly to gain employment in an effort to provide for her.

We see many couples where the wife has a larger

income than her husband. This doesn't mean that you are not creating financial security. This is where steward-ship and wisdom can increase her security even if you are not providing the lion's share of the income. Knowing that you will ensure that she always has a home, food, and her basics needs, will ensure that her need for finan-cial security is met.

What are some practical ways that you can meet each of the different types of security needs for her?

Him:

_____

_____

_____

_____

_____

_____

_____

_____

_____

_____

_____

_____

_____

What are some ways that your spouse could help you become more secure in each of these areas?

Her:

_____

_____

_____

_____

_____

_____

_____

_____

_____

_____

_____

_____

_____

_____

_____

_____

_____

_____

_____

_____

_____

_____

The second most important need of women is affection. Affection often means very different things to men and to women. Affection is defined in the dictionary as a tender feeling towards one another. Often this can also be identified as non-sexual touch. Affection can also be the expression of care. It symbolizes protection, comfort and approval. When spouses are affectionate towards one another it sends the following messages: 'You are important to me and I will care for and protect you.' 'I am concerned about the problems you face and will be there for you when you need me.' Affection comes naturally during the dating process. However, affection becomes more important in the marriage because it says that you are still valuable and worth being pursued.

It is always better to be over affectionate than under affectionate. In doing this you will eliminate any doubt about your feelings. Frequent simple gestures of kindness and physical touch are great ways to meet the need for affection. Hand holding, sitting with your arm around her, a kiss or just the act of a gentle touch without any need for this to lead to sex are important in ensuring that her need for affection is fully satisfied Non-sexual touch fosters the sense of companionship in a couple.

Additionally such things as a kind word, a greeting card, a text message or a love note unexpectedly tucked into her purse are always great ways to demonstrate affection. The ultimate goal is to make sure that she always knows that she is on your mind.

I (Melisa) have found from time to time that Steven has an amazing ability to be extremely affectionate. I personally can, at times, become a little claustrophobic when people are in my personal space too much. Steven had to learn the balance of meeting my need for affection versus overwhelming me with his affection. Learning balance in this area is important . The husband ability to realize and appreciate his wife's comfort level will only serve to strengthen their relationship.

Provide several examples of ways you can demonstrate affection in marriage.

The third need of a woman is open communication. Conversation, not in generalities, but with details and emotion attached. Most men will need to make a concerted effort to meet their wives needs in this area. Women are generally freer to express emotion and details when communicating with others.

Men generally have a tendency to communicate precisely and matter-of-factly. Men need to develop their communication skills to meet this need of their wives. It is only in some areas where they struggle. For example, when a man is telling another man about a car, he can communicate make, model, horsepower, engine size, and details without difficulty. Husbands need to utilize that same type of communication in order to meet the communication needs of his wife. He does this both by listening to her and by mapping out the details of his heart.

Husbands, if you feel that your wife is bombarding you with questions, this is a good indicator that you are not adequately meeting her communication needs. By providing conversation in sentences not one-word answers you will find that the barrage of questions may subside. By making a commitment to conversation you will take the fear out of hearing her say, "We need to talk."

By being an active participant in conversation, even starting them at times, you are building your marriage, meeting her need, and drawing closer together.

Remember that body language is a huge part of communication. Talking to her while acting like you are going to the dentist is not relaying that you feel it is important to her. It conveys you are doing it because you have to. A gift not freely given is not really a gift. Give her the gift of communication, she will treasure it.

Guys, provide the details of your day:

_____

_____

_____

_____

_____

_____

_____

_____

_____

_____

_____

_____

_____

_____

_____

Ladies ask open questions that encourage him to provide the details and emotions you need to hear:

_____

_____

_____

_____

_____

_____

_____

_____

_____

_____

The fourth primary need of women is leadership. Leadership is not domination. Leadership is the act of getting others to willingly follow. Men are called to be the leaders of the home in many areas. Spiritual leadership is the most important area. Spiritual leadership involves Bible reading/study, prayer, and church involvement. Leadership is provided by example more than verbal directive. Leadership should also be demonstrated in the areas of finances, romance, and children. Wives need to provide an environment where men can remain in the leadership role that God has designed for them. It is important for women to be submitted to the leadership of their husbands. This can be difficult if a woman comes from a home where her father did not assume his leadership role or where a mother dominated the relationship. This will be an area where women with strong personalities may struggle. The benefit of strong leadership will be a clearly defined purpose and direction. This will enable the couple to work together as a unit and accomplish more in their relationship. When wives will allow their husbands the opportunity to assume his role as leader, they will see God's blessing on their marriage in amazing ways.

Christ is the undisputed leader of the church and the Bible specifically directs husbands to follow His example of leadership. The concept that the husband is the head of the home is laid out very clearly in Ephesians 5:23 *"For the husband is the head of the wife as Christ is the head of the church, his body, of which he is the Savior."*

To replicate Christ's leadership in the marriage, let's take a look at who and how Christ leads. Christ led his disciples and in a defining moment of leadership he chose to serve them by washing their feet. (John 13:1-17) In the middle of this passage Peter tries to refuse Christ's service and as the ultimate servant/leader, Jesus convinces

Peter that His service is necessary. For great leadership to exist, great service needs to be present. What better role can we take than the same that Christ had done himself, as a leader with a deep sense of humility?

In Philippians 2:7 Christ's surrendering heaven to become a man provides the ultimate example of sacrificial love an essential component in marital leadership. The art of having people follow you out of love will almost always involve self-sacrifice. When you are dating how often do you ask her to pay? It was easy to sacrifice your money and your free time all for her. You should always remember that a husband's willingness to sacrifice will encourage his wife's willingness to follow his leadership.

1. What are ways you, as the husband, can demonstrate leadership in each of these areas (security, affection, communication, and spiritual leadership)?

_____

_____

_____

_____

_____

_____

_____

_____

_____

_____

_____

_____

_____

2. As a wife, what are some actions that you can use to demonstrate you are willing to allow you husband to lead?

_____

_____

_____

_____

_____

_____

_____

_____

_____

_____

_____

_____

_____

_____

CONFLICT RESOLUTION

Marriage without conflict is not possible. The Bible says in 1 Corinthians 7:28 – *"He who marries will have trouble in this life."* While this is not the scripture that you hear quoted at many weddings, it is in fact a very true statement.

Conflict, however, doesn't necessarily mean anger. Conflict in a relationship is something that can be used to help spur growth in the individuals involved if it is handled properly. It can also be something that wounds and causes damage to the heart of one or both of the people involved. In conflict resolution you can look at it as either a tug of war or as give and take.

One way is confrontational, with a clear winner and loser. The other way is based in compromise, where both sides get something out of it. There are many ways to deal with conflict when it arises in marriage. Often times the way we deal with conflict is either very similar to the way we saw conflict handled by our family/parents or completely the opposite.

I (Melisa) was raised in a home where my mother and father didn't have a lot of conflict. This was primarily due to the fact that my mother avoided it. Her motto was that it takes two people to fight and if one of them isn't fighting, then the other one runs out of steam pretty quickly. She didn't see being right as something that was very important and therefore, was very willing to adapt to whatever my father wanted. She did, however, on a rare occasion, hold her ground if she thought there was something very important at stake. Because she so rarely took a stand, my father was pretty quick to get into agreement with her when she did, so I came from a family where there was not a lot of conflict between my parents. This didn't mean that I didn't have conflict with my dad, I did, and often times it was very unproductive for me. I learned that conflict rarely ended the way I wanted it to, so it didn't have a lot of appeal for me.

In my first marriage I learned that conflict was always accompanied by increased decibels. It was also occasionally accompanied by flying objects and harsh words. This reinforced my belief that conflict was HIGHLY overrated and I learned to avoid is at all costs.

I (Steven) grew up in a house where conflict was a

battle of wits. Almost nobody ever yelled or screamed, but you knew you had crossed someone when the insults started flying, and then it was on. It rarely resulted in one side surrendering, and it almost always resulted in somebody getting his or her feelings hurt. This is usually the case when every altercation involves proving you were better, smarter, or more correct.

When we got together, the birds chirped, the angels sang, and there was peace all around, for a while. In fact, Steven's mother was very concerned that we had not had a fight prior to our wedding. However, in an attempt to reassure her, we had our first fight the night before our wedding, and it was kind of a doozy. Probably because we were both tired and there had been some significant conflict between Steven and his brother, we were ripe for an argument. I (Melisa) had gotten Steven a new cross necklace for a wedding gift. As we sat in the floor of our bedroom, I was thrilled to present him with this token of my great love for him. He opened it, looked at it, and said thanks. I thought my heartfelt choosing of the perfect wedding gift would net me copious amounts of praise, and all I got was "thank you." Needless to say, my feelings were trampled on and the crying started. Steven was angry because he thought "thank you" was an appropriate response, and that was where expectations and emotions collided. I got my feelings hurt, Steve got defensive, and we got introduced to arguing for the first time. The honeymoon was officially over and we hadn't even gotten married yet.

What did you learn from your parents about how to handle conflict? Is this the approach that you use to handle conflict? Does it usually go well or poorly?

Him:

_____

_____

_____

_____

_____

_____

_____

_____

_____

Her:

_____

_____

_____

_____

_____

_____

_____

_____

_____

_____

With the enormity of the next day's events, we quickly got over ourselves and had a wonderful, beautiful wedding. Getting over yourself leads us to our next point.

Frequently, conflict is caused by selfishness. We often find ourselves in conflict because we have a desire to have the other person do what we want them to do. The attitude where you feel it's necessary to get your way invites the spirit of division into the relationship. When we can stop ourselves in the middle of a conversation and try to determine if selfishness is driving the conflict, we are better able to re-frame our expectations and see resolutions that will be beneficial to both parties.

Philippians 2:3-4 says, *"Do nothing from selfishness or empty conceit, but with humility of mind regard one another as more important than yourselves; do not merely look out for your own personal interests, but also for the interests of others."*

This gives a great example of how to treat other people in general. Luke 9:23 reminds us that in order to follow Christ, we must deny ourselves and take up our cross daily. This scripture gives us a framework of how to view ourselves. When you combine these two Biblical blueprints, it allows you to uproot selfishness and gives you the upper hand in creating a peaceful solution to your conflicts.

When we empty ourselves of selfishness and allow God to fill us up with love, we find that conflict resolution comes much quicker.

In 1 Corinthians 13:4-8 we see a list of what love is and what love isn't. *"Love is patient, love is kind and is not jealous; love does not brag and is not arrogant, does not act unbecomingly; it does not seek its own, is not provoked, does not take into account a wrong suffered, does not rejoice in unrighteousness, but rejoices with the truth; bears all things, believes all things, hopes all things, endures all things. Love never fails."*

This passage is often read at weddings and with good reason. As we read this passage, we see the very definition of love. Walking in love is the key to successful conflict resolution. When in conflict, both parties have the right to provide input, but they must do so in a loving and respectful way. Love can accomplish more towards ending a fight than any cleverly constructed argument can.

Describe two or three ways that you can utilize love in conflict resolution.

Him

_____

_____

_____

_____

_____

_____

_____

_____

_____

_____

_____

_____

_____

_____

_____

_____

_____

_____

Her

_____

_____

_____

_____

_____

_____

_____

_____

_____

_____

_____

_____

_____

_____

_____

_____

_____

_____

_____

_____

_____

_____

Forgiveness is vital in conflict resolution. Resolving conflict doesn't happen if one or both of the people involved are unwilling to forgive. Withholding forgiveness is the acid that eats away at a successful long-term resolution. Forgiveness neutralizes that acid and promotes long-term stability. At the end of a conflict, you must come to a place where any forgiveness needed has been provided. This is crucial to ultimately having conflict resolution. Forgiveness also means that there is no score keeping.

1 Corinthians 13:5 reminds us that love takes no account of wrongs done to it. When one or both people become historical, (and/or hysterical) during conflict, resolution is either very delayed or not possible. By choosing to forgive, you bring the conflict to a place where resolution is possible.

Matthew 6:14-15 says *"For if you forgive others for their transgressions, your heavenly Father will also forgive you. But if you do not forgive others, then your Father will not forgive your transgressions."*

Not only does forgiveness help you in the sweet by and by, but it provides immeasurable benefits in the nasty here and now. If it helps you now and it helps you later, there is no reason not to incorporate it immediately so you can start reaping the benefits immediately.

There are several ways to prevent or quickly resolve

conflict in a marriage. These simple techniques, when utilized, invite the spirit of unity and bring glory to God. The first is to be quiet. Let the other person talk. Sincerely consider what your spouse is trying to say. Try not to counter an idea before you have allowed it to be fully presented. When you listen intentionally to what your spouse is saying and allow them to fully present their position without thinking about your response when they are talking, it will help prevent you from jumping to unnecessary or inaccurate conclusions.

James 1:19-20 tells us to be quick to listen, slow to speak, and slow to become angry, for a man's anger does not bring about the righteous life that God desires. This may be difficult for some, but is a habit worth forming.

Proverbs 15:18 says, *"A hot-tempered man stirs up dissension but a patient man calms a quarrel."* By not allowing your spouse to fully present their position and by interrupting them, you often create unnecessary arguments.

The second technique is to be still. This is similar to being quiet, but is not the same thing. Being still allows you time to consider the other side. It also gives God the opportunity to speak to your situation.

Psalm 46:10 says *"Be still and know that I am God."* God is a gentleman and won't interrupt. When you take time to be still, you allow the Holy Spirit to infuse discernment into what you are about to say. This will promote peace and prevent hurt feelings from harmful and injuring words.

Proverbs 15:1 says, *"A quiet answer deflects anger but harsh words make tempers flare."* When you take the opportunity to be still and respond quietly and peacefully, you invite a peaceful resolution. One thing to recognize is that being still is not a license to isolate your spouse. There is a difference between taking time to consider the other person's position and providing a measured, loving, and respectful response versus giving the other person the cold shoulder or putting them in the penalty box. Withholding communication is not conflict resolution. It just delays dealing with a conflict.

The third technique is to always be respectful. Often we see people have a tendency to be disrespectful when they are angry. They speak in a disrespectful tone or use disrespectful words. Disrespect doesn't have to be loud or angry, but it can be delivered in a matter of fact tone and malicious intent through the use of sarcasm.

I (Steven) grew up in a house where we never raised our voices to each other, but engaged routinely in bouts of verbal one-upmanship with sarcasm as our primary weapon. Having been raised with sarcasm, it was mother's milk to me, and just like mother's milk, I needed to be weaned off of it. You can choose your words to inflict the most damage or to do the most good, but either way it is still a choice. An argument doesn't get resolved by attrition, by vanquishing a foe. You can undo a lot of flowery words if your tone and body language indicate they are insincere. An icy apology through gritted teeth communicates the opposite of "I'm sorry."

Not only aren't you sorry, but a clenched jaw shows you are unwilling to budge from your position. By making sure that your body language, words, and tone of voice all communicate respect that will prevent unnecessary hurt and an escalation of the conflict. Choosing to act and speak in a respectful way invites peace and resolution and allows the other person to feel heard and understood.

The fourth technique is using acknowledgments in conflict. Using statements that acknowledge that you have heard the other person and validate their position brings about a quicker resolution from a calmer place. Acknowledging statements might include: "I see where you're coming from," "That's a good point," "I can see that," "I can understand where you got that from what I said." These are just a few of the types of statements that indicate you are still actively listening to the other person.

It also demonstrates your willingness to see their point of view. You can also try to paraphrase what the person is saying to show your understanding of their side of the argument.

You can start off these statements with "So what you're saying is…" and then reiterating what their position is in your own words. If you are off-base in your assumption, this gives the other party the opportunity to explain what they are trying to convey in a way you can understand better. You always want to make sure that your acknowledging statements are sincere and from the heart so that they promote peace. If they come across as condescending, they will more likely just pour gas on the fire of an already volatile conversation.

The fifth technique is asking clarifying questions. Unfortunately, we don't all come into conversations or conflicts from the same perspective. Asking clarifying questions such as, "Can you help with that?" or "Can you tell me more about that?" lets the other person know they have been heard and it allows you to get more information on the table so both sides can find a resolution easier. Much like stillness and quietness work together, acknowledging statements and clarifying questions work together.

Clarifying questions transmit value by saying to the other person, "I want to understand you correctly." By giving value at the beginning of the conflict, it helps promote security and safety, which in turn leads to calm solutions.

3. Rank the five conflict resolution techniques from hardest for you to easiest. and give examples of ways to use these techniques in resolving conflict.

Him:

_____

_____

_____

_____

_____

_____

_____

_____

_____

_____

_____

_____

_____

_____

_____

_____

_____

Her:

_____

_____

_____

_____

_____

_____

_____

_____

_____

_____

_____

_____

_____

_____

_____

_____

_____

_____

_____

_____

_____

The Greatest Wedding Present Ever

Keeping in mind we are building around the idea of a God-centered marriage, when we look at sex, let's take a look at what God says about it. One thing we want to do is to re-frame how people think about sex and the Bible, God's guidebook for everything including sex. So to do that, let's look at what the Bible says about stripper poles. Take a moment and give that some thought. If you came up with nothing, you are absolutely right. There is nothing in the Bible about stripper poles. About the only thing you can take away from that is if you have one you'd better be married to the one using the pole and it should be in your home.

There are many misconceptions about what God says about sex in the Bible and we hope to dispel them in this chapter. It is God who created sex. It gets better than that. Everything He creates is good, and He gave it to us.

By us, I mean married couples. The do's and don'ts of sex can be found primarily but not exclusively in a couple of places. A lot of the don'ts are found in Leviticus chapter 18. Don't throw it out just because it's Old Testament, it's in the Bible for a reason. Before you get too wound up about the 47 biblical rules you're about to get that'll suck the joy out of your sex life, let's take a closer look.

What the Bible actually speaks against are for the most part things that society, and not just Christians, frown upon: don't sleep with your mom or step-mom, brothers and sisters, nieces and nephews, brothers- and sisters-in-law, neighbors, same sex partners, and no animals. Not a lot of outside the box thinking here. It leaves an awful lot that is allowable. This is why sex is one of God's most wonderful gifts.

God never does anything without a purpose and sex is no different. The first reason behind it is to forge a covenant between a man and a woman. Gen 2 :24 *"For this reason a man will leave his father and mother and be united to his wife and the two shall become one flesh."* A covenant is about surrendering your rights and assuming your responsibilities.

The world is all about the marriage contract. Contracts have the reverse effect. They are about protecting your rights and limiting your responsibilities. This is displayed by the increasing use of prenuptial contracts. Now a days you don't even have to be the ultra wealthy to go into a marriage looking to "protect what's yours." That attitude already limits your ability to become one flesh because you are withholding. Sex is the only activity that is 100% exclusive to a husband and wife. You will eventually do almost everything else with someone else. Praying, laughing, eating, working, and going to church are all great and all are better with other people. Sex is like the great toy you got for Christmas and didn't want to share with your brothers and sisters. The best thing about it you don't have to and shouldn't share it.

The next reason God created sex is procreation. The bonus round of great sex is you get to have kids, and eventually grandkids. There is nothing better than a happy baby face. As proud grandparents we can attest to that. Children are an amazing blessing. God allows us to double dip in the pleasure department with sex and kids.

The directive is simple, and spelled out in Genesis 1:27-28 *"So God created mankind in his own image, in the image of God He created them: male and female He created them. God blessed them and said to them, be fruitful and increase in number to fill the earth and subdue it."* It's simple, straightforward, and from God.

The third reason, and we saved the best for last, is for pleasure. Yes, I said it, God wants up to have great, satisfying, and pleasure-filled sex into our golden years. How do we know this? All you have to do is go to the Song of Solomon. From its opening verses in chapter 1:2 *"Let him kiss me with the kisses of his mouth- for your love is more delightful than any wine'*, to 1:4 *"Take me away with you – let us hurry! Let the king bring me to his chamber."* All the way through the final verse in 8:14 *"Come away, my lover, and be like a gazelle or like a young stag on the spice laden mountains."* Throughout the entire book 8 chapters he paints a picture of passion, beauty, and yes, of sex from courtship through marriage to the honeymoon bed, as God intended it. Sometimes it's more symbolic speaking of gazelles, spices, and fruits other times it takes almost no imagination, talking about kissing or saying this is my lover.

The original intent of God was for a husband and wife to live together without shame. When God created Adam and Eve in the garden there was no sense of shame. Genesis 1:25. However, we note that after the introduction of sin into their lives, shame followed.

This is detailed in Genesis 3:7-10 *"Then the eyes of both of them were opened, and they realized they were naked; so they sewed fig leaves together and made coverings for themselves. Then the man and his wife heard the sound of the Lord God as he was walking in the garden in the cool of the day, and they hid from the Lord God among the trees of the garden. But the Lord God called to the man, "Where are you?" He answered, "I heard you in the garden, and I was afraid because I was naked; so I hid."*

It is interesting to note here that they sewed fig leaves to cover their genitals. This was the original indicator of the entrance of shame. One of the best ways to avoid attaching shame to sex in your marriage is to always be diligent to treat your spouse in a respectful way. Respect is the antidote to shame. There are several ways to demonstrate respect for your spouse in regards to sex. Some of the best ways to show respect are as follows:

1. **Respect your spouse's boundaries:**
   Creativity in the bedroom is wonderful. It generates excitement and expectation, all the while preventing boredom. However, when any area of creativity causes your spouse to feel uncomfortable or shamed in any way, it is important to be sensitive to this. It is NOT okay to cross any boundary your spouse has. They also need to feel totally okay to saying no without any repercussions. No still means no, cliché or not.

2. **Respect each person sexual history:**
   Our history involves more than just how many previous partners we've had. The attitude towards

sex we were raised with contributes to our history as well. A person's sexual history should never be used as a weapon against them. This includes the tendency to compare them to previous partners. Prior sexual sins are just that, prior. What's in the past shouldn't be dredged up to put your spouse in a negative or shameful light. If your spouse has repented, that is good enough for God and it should be good enough for you. We don't dwell in the past, we learn from it.

3. **Respect your spouse's desire for sex:**
We want to remind you that sex is God's idea, His gift, His creation. You should never make your spouse feel guilty for wanting sex. Sex drive is built into all of us, just to varying degrees. If your husband/wife wants sex more, or for that matter less, you need to respect that.

Being able to talk openly and honestly about sex is vital. Open communication will reduce the opportunity for shame to attach itself to sex during marriage, it will allow a husband and wife to embrace it without fear. In some cases it will be a new experience for one or both of you. It's an exciting path you can walk down together. You need to establish solid communication in the area of sex to prevent hurt and resentment, as well as shame from taking up residence in your marriage bed.

Discuss any boundaries you feel will be needed to help ensure you are comfortable and respectful of each other, once you are married.

_____

_____

_____

_____

_____

_____

_____

_____

_____

_____

_____

_____

_____

_____

_____

_____

_____

_____

_____

Speaking of the marriage bed, scripture specifically deals with purity inside marriage. Hebrews 13:4 states, "Marriage should be honored by all and the marriage bed kept pure, for God will judge the adulterer and all the sexually immoral." It sounds so simple looking at it from the early stage of marriage.

Keep in mind the words of Jesus in Matthew 5:28, *"But I tell you that anyone who looks at a woman lustfully has already committed adultery with her in his heart."* You are going to have a truly fulfilling sex life when you able to honor the marriage bed in both thought and deed. This is not to say we have to walk through life staring at the ground for fear of seeing an attractive member of the opposite sex and violating Christ's directions. It is to remind us to be mentally disciplined enough not to dwell or fantasize about it as we protect the sanctity of our marriage beds.

This gets harder and harder to do with the bombardment of sexual images and the rampant availability of pornography in society today. A common misconception about pornography is it is not adultery because there is no physical interaction, and no one gets hurt because there is no violence.

This couldn't be further from the truth. The words of Christ dispel the ideas about adultery. The violence is emotional and the hurt is very real and deep for the spouse of the pornography user. Many times people who engage in ongoing use of pornography develop a distorted sense of sexual priorities. Pornography becomes their most important sexual relationship overtaking their sexual relationship with their spouse. For many, the relationship with pornography is developed in adolescence and continues into adulthood.

This long- term relationship causes a pattern of destruction that repeats itself as long as the relationship remains intact. It is vital that the relationship with pornography ends completely. Stopping usage first requires going to God with a repentant heart. No long-term solution will remain in place on man's strength alone. By white-knuckling it, you are setting yourself up for failure.

There is a warning in Proverbs 26:11, *"Like a dog returns to its vomit is a fool who repeats his folly."* Many times the shame of pornography usage prevents people from seeking help. To repeat patterns that have been unsuccessful in the past is to live out the warning in Proverbs. Another saying is, repeating the same behavior while expecting different results is the definition of insanity. After going to God, you must be brave enough to seek spiritual guidance and accountability from people who have had success in this area. By involving others in the healing process, it reduces the powerful hold that secret can have.

There are two scriptures that speak specifically to this idea. James 5:16, *"Therefore confess your sins one to another and pray for each other that you may be healed. The prayer of a righteous man is powerful and effective."*

Also, Ephesians 5:8-14, *"For you were once in darkness, but now you are in the light in the Lord. Live as children of the light (for the fruit of the light consists in all goodness, righteousness, and truth) and find out what pleases the Lord. Have nothing to do with the fruitless deeds of darkness, but rather expose them. For it is shameful even to mention what the disobedient do in secret. But everything exposed by the light becomes visible, for the light makes everything visible."*

By releasing the powerful hold of this secret you will be able to bring healing and restoration to your sexual relationship with your spouse.

There is a subtler disobedience in how we address our spouse in the bedroom. There are two sets of needs that should always be addressed in healthy marital sex. You can often become absorbed in your needs, wants, and desires. This can let selfishness creep in. As we discussed in the conflict resolution chapter selfishness is the root of many conflicts. Conflict in the bedroom can lead to only sleeping in the bedroom. There are very few marriages that can survive that.

Selfish sex is ungodly sex. God's design for sex is

further laid out in 1 Corinthians 7:3-5, *"The husband should fulfill his martial duty to his wife, and likewise the wife to her husband. The wife does not have authority over her own body but yields it to her husband. In the same way, the husband does not have over his own body but yields it to his wife. Do not deprive each other except perhaps by mutual consent and for a time, so that you may devote yourself to prayer. Then come together again so that Satan will not tempt you because of your lack of self-control."*

Sex is such a powerful tool in making great marriages. Satan will seek to turn it against marriages. How do we keep Satan out of our bedrooms? The same way we keep him out of everywhere else, with prayer. This is a revolutionary concept when it comes to sex. You don't keep God out of your kitchen or dining room. Many times on a cold Minnesota day I have prayed that my car would start. There isn't a big red circle with a slash through it that prevents God from seeing what's going on in your bedroom.

Welcome God into your sex life. It's His idea after all. Try praying before sex, sounds funky, but give it a shot. Then afterwards, you can thank Him for the best wedding present ever. You'll find yielding to and seeking God in your sex life will allow you to reap all the benefits found in the Song of Solomon. You will also be strengthened in the areas where the enemy may try to attack your sexual integrity. From chapter one, we talked about God being at the center of your marriage. You'll find everything is better when you involve God in it, especially sex.

MONEY! MONEY! MONEY!

One of the most often misquoted Scripture passages is 1 Timothy 6:10. It is often quoted as, "Money is the root of all evil." Actually the Scripture says, *"For the love of money is a root of all kinds of evil." Emphasis mine.*

In the society we live in today, the love of money is seen almost everywhere you look. From the professional athletes to the multimillionaire businessmen like Donald Trump. It seems that everyone in the United States is busy chasing the "almighty" dollar. Christians, for the most part, are not much different in that aspect. While money is important and we need it to live, how we manage it in a marriage is more important.

Before you say the "I Do's", keeping your money separate is the best approach. However, after the ring is on the finger, it's time to join your assets. Because of the very high incidence of divorce in our country, we have seen the increase of prenuptial agreements and separate bank accounts. By joining your money, however, you are not starting the marriage with the idea that if this goes badly I can just take MY money and leave.

There are many topics to cover when it comes to finances in marriage, so let's get first things first. First of all, money is important. In fact, the Bible talks more about money than it does about faith. It can be the source of great blessings or the source of what some people would consider a curse. The Bible is very clear about the way to ensure that blessings flow into your life through money.

6 "I the Lord do not change. So you, the descendants of Jacob, are not destroyed. 7 Ever since the time of your ancestors you have turned away from my decrees and have not kept them. Return to me, and I will return to you," says the Lord Almighty. "But you ask, 'How are we to return?' 8 "Will a mere mortal rob God? Yet you rob me. "But you ask, 'How are we robbing you?' "In tithes and offerings. 9 You are under a curse — your whole nation— because you are robbing me. 10 Bring the whole tithe into the storehouse, that there may be food in my house. Test me in this," says the Lord Almighty, "and see if I will not throw open the floodgates of heaven and pour out so much blessing that there will not be room enough to store it. 11 I will prevent pests from devour-

ing your crops, and the vines in your fields will not drop their fruit before it is ripe, " says the Lord Almighty. **12** *"Then all the nations will call you blessed, for yours will be a delightful land," says the Lord Almighty (Malachi 3:6-12).*

Just like sex is the covenant between a husband and wife, tithing is the covenant between you and God. It is important to establish, prior to marriage, that tithing will be a non-negotiable in your marriage. Tithing refers to giving God the first ten percent of your income. That includes paychecks, sales, gifts, and any other way the money finds its way to you. By ensuring agreement on tithing, you are ensuring that God will provide His blessing. The Bible is clear that not only will God provide increase, He will also rebuke the devourer for your sake. This is why tithing is paramount in finances. When you commit to tithing BEFORE you're married, you start your marriage off with the blessings of God in place.

When we first met online, we spent many hours talking on the phone. When I (Melisa) brought up tithing, Steven was not really interested in giving his money to the church. He thought it was better to give his time to the church as his tithe, and after all, he occasionally plunked $10 in the bucket.

I proceeded to tell Steven that tithing wasn't optional and that it was how we demonstrated obedience to God. I will never forget the next statement he made, "Well, I will have to have a scriptural directive to do that." Oddly enough, I was able to rattle off about 3 or 4 scriptures that talk about tithing such as Deuteronomy 26:12, Malachi 3:10, Luke 20:22-25. Being a man of his word, Steven saw the "scriptural directive" and began to tithe.

Offerings are different from tithes. Offerings are monies that you give in addition to the tithe. These are great and should be done as God guides you to do so. It is important, however, to decide how much of an offering can be made without the agreement of your spouse. Setting a limit on the size of the offering to be given is a great way to ensure that conflict will not arise.

What has been your previous experience with tithing and giving offerings? Will you commit to tithe in your marriage?

Him:

_____

_____

_____

_____

_____

_____
_____
_____
_____
_____

Her:

_____
_____
_____
_____
_____
_____
_____
_____
_____
_____

Communication in marriage where it relates to finances is crucial. By starting your marriage with openness about where you are in your finances and committing to being transparent about spending, you will have better success in managing your finances and your marriage.

Although you may share a bank account, the two of you are both separate spending entities. In this sense, the left hand must know what the right hand is doing. Communicating with each other about spending and sharing a commitment to a budget is the best thing for keeping financial stability.

When we began to get serious about our relationship and knew that getting married was God's plan for our lives, I (Steven) decided that Melisa should know exactly where I stood as far as my finances were concerned. On a trip to Oklahoma, I brought along a canvas book bag. Much to her dismay, this bag did not include a gift for her or any of her children, but it did include a big surprise.

Feeling compelled to be honest and open about my wealth, or lack of it, I revealed the contents of the bag to her. I dumped on her floor three and a half months worth of credit card bills, phone bills, gym membership bills, many of which weren't even opened and two thirds of which weren't paid. I had never been good at math, so budgeting did not come easy. Rather than learn it, I ignored it and reaped what I sowed.

I (Melisa) must admit that I was shocked to see his lack of money management. However, because we were still in the 'love is blind' phase of our relationship, I was certain that this was not going to be a problem. Luckily for me, Steven is a man of character and chose to do what was best for his soon to be family. We organized the bills and developed a plan to deal with them. So if you find yourself in this kind of situation, it is far better in the long run to be honest and open and begin to correct any problems before you get married.

One of the best ways to develop transparency in spending is by utilizing a budget and a daily accounting of your spending. This allows for everyone to know where the money is going and prevents the inclination of hiding expenditures.

Many have heard the idea about women buying clothes, purses and shoes and then hiding them in the closet until a later date only to be able to say they have had them for "a long time." This kind of deception in finances is very hazardous to your marriage. By understanding that secrets have a devastating power when they are revealed, it is far better to not have them to start with.

By starting the marriage with a clear budget and an agreement to stay in the budget, you will be able to build long-term success in your finances. It is important to pray about major decisions, especially in spending. This allows for God to be involved in the decision making process and will many times prevent rash and impulsive spending.

In what ways will you utilize budgeting and daily accountability for spending in your marriage?

Him:

_____

_____

_____

_____

_____

_____

_____

Her:

_____

_____

_____

_____

_____

_____

_____

_____

_____

Often in marriage you will find that one of the spouses is a spender and one will be a saver. This can cause conflict if you don't identify ahead of time how your money will be spent. You may also find that one of the spouses is better with managing money (i.e. number crunching) than the other. This is a great time to utilize the particular gifts that are available to your marriage.

While the husband is the head of the family, it doesn't necessarily mean he has to be the one who actually balances the checkbook and pays the bills if the wife is better at it. It does mean, however, that whoever pays the bills and balances the bank accounts needs to be open and willing to review these with their spouse.

It is also important to discuss the idea of blow money or allowances. It is important in the marriage to provide each spouse with a previously decided upon amount of money that is theirs to spend however they wish. This allows for each one to be able to not feel like they have to justify every purchase they make. If the husband wants to buy games for his gaming system but the wife feels this is a waste of money, using his blow money for games allows him to feel like he can have something he wants and her to not feel like he is wasting the household budget money.

The same is true for women who enjoy shopping for clothes, purses, jewelry, and shoes. The wife has the freedom to purchase the things she desires without having to feel guilty. This allows for the freedom to spend money, but it also allows the freedom to spend money without the feeling of judgment. There is no stupid use of blow money. Providing a judgment-free atmosphere allows your spouse to feel that you love them whatever their idiosyncrasies may be.

Dave Ramsey says, "Money is fun...if you have some." It is especially true when it comes to the next topic related to finances, debt. Debt can be one of the most destructive forces within a marriage and is one of the primary reasons cited for divorce in this country. Especially early on in marriage, debt may be hard to avoid, and if you come into the marriage with debt it will be something that you have to learn to deal with. Debt needs to be a house guest that will eventually leave and not become a life long member of the family. If you are starting out your marriage without any debt, then it will be easier to maintain a life without it. Learning to live within your means will be one of the best things you can do to ensure marital success.

I (Melisa) have a quote that I learned many years from my spiritual father. He would always say, "When your outgo exceeds your income, your upkeep will become your downfall." This is a timeless truth that is worth heeding.

Many times people get caught up in the trap of "keeping up with the Jones'." This causes many people to justify the idea of purchasing things by going into debt to get them. This concept, along with the idea many young people have that they should immediately start out their marriage with the same standard of living that their parents have achieved after working for many years can be a very dangerous place to be.

Being willing to forgo a few luxuries until you can pay cash for them is not always fun, it is a great way to decrease your financial burdens in the future. By not spending tomorrow's earnings today, you will find that your marriage is set up for success. By decreasing your financial burdens you decrease the burdens in your marriage, which is less weight for everyone to bear.

God knows the destructive power debt has on people and He provides us with this knowledge through His word. Proverbs 22:7 talks about "the borrower being subject to the lender," and Romans 13:8 says, *"we should owe no man anything but to love them."* The great thing about owing no man anything, but to love him is that love doesn't charge interest and earns a great return on your investment.

One of the great lies about finances is the dependence on your credit and FICA scores. If you are choosing to live a life with debt, then your credit and FICA scores are important. However, if you choose to live a life free of debt and pay cash for what you buy, then these two numbers are completely irrelevant. The only way to build your credit score is to borrow money. This completely defeats the idea of paying cash for your purchases. Debt brings with it interest, which causes you to pay more for what you are buying than what it is really worth. Saving to buy what you want is a way to make interest.

Also, paying cash will frequently get you a better deal. By current standards, if you purchase a house with a mortgage you will find you are paying more than twice the price for it with the interest you are required to pay. If you purchase a new vehicle with credit, you are going to lose twenty percent of the value when you drive off the lot. You would never borrow money to purchase stocks that are guaranteed to lose twenty percent of the value of the stock.

What is the clear picture of your current financial status?

Him:

_____

_____

_____

_____

_____

_____

_____

_____

_____

_____

Her:

_____

_____

_____

_____

_____

_____

_____

_____

What is your plan to minimize or eliminate debt in your marriage?

Him:

_____

_____

_____

_____

_____

_____

_____

_____

_____

_____

Her:

_____

_____

_____

_____

_____

_____

_____

The final topic to be addressed is stewardship. Stewardship can be defined as the responsible planning and use of resources. When you embrace the idea that God is the master of your life and everything you have belongs to Him, it makes becoming a good steward of your resources much easier.

By wisdom a house is built and through understanding it is established; through knowledge its rooms are filled with rare and beautiful treasures (Proverbs 24:3-4).

With proper stewardship of the resources God has provided us, we will ensure that we can survive in both prosperous and difficult financial climates. A great Biblical example of this kind of stewardship is the story of Joseph. It's in the story of Joseph that we see the combination of knowledge, divine inspiration and resources in a classic example of stewardship guiding Egypt from prosperity through famine and back to prosperity (Genesis 41).

Stewardship is the final piece of the financial puzzle and by employing the concepts previously discussed you will see proper stewardship of your resources.

What do you see in the Bible regarding stewardship that you can utilize in the management of your resources?

Him:

_____

_____

_____

_____

_____

_____

_____

_____

Her:

_____

_____

_____

_____

_____

_____

_____

_____

Kids and Family!
All For 1 and 1 For All

When you purchase a new deck of cards, all the suits are separated as well as the numbers being perfectly in order. This is a great representation of families prior to the wedding. Once the couple has joined into the covenant relationship of marriage, the deck gets shuffled. The merging of two families is exactly how God designed it. However, in this era, it can be one of the hardest things to do. With families that are very mobile and less traditional it can become a difficult task at times. In today's society with the preponderance of blended families, sometimes it's like shuffling two or three decks at once. By simply developing a plan prior to the wedding, you can avoid some of the traps that many couples find themselves in.

A top priority in successfully joining two families

starts with each person being very intentional about building a relationship with their spouse's family. This is the first key in the successful shuffling of the cards, so to speak. It requires both spouses to work together to help identify the unique characteristics of their own family. Each of you must become a student of your spouse's family. While learning something new is at times difficult, you have a wonderful gift. You have a tutor that has many years of experience with the family you are learning about. By working together, this process can be smooth and pleasant.

Some of the important details that should be learned include: family expectations of time spent together, holiday traditions, religious beliefs and practices, and other unique family expectations. Today's society where more and more people are on their second and third marriages may make this more difficult, but it will also allow for a wider variety of experience and traditions to be drawn from. While it is not possible to always accommodate all the traditions of both families, talking about those traditions with each other and developing a plan and presenting that plan to your families before the wedding, you will be able to eliminate a significant amount of stress and hurt feelings after the wedding.

Because in most cases every family wants to have some input into the wedding, this is a great opportunity to expand the conversation to future family traditions and expectations, thereby allowing you to honor both families' traditions while establishing new traditions for your own family.

I (Melisa) was raised in a very conservative home. My parents were very nearly teetotalers. I, having grown up in a Southern Baptist church, thought people who drank were not in a relationship with Christ. Yes, I get that this is very Pharisaical, but that was my belief. I spent most of my life living by this religious code. Then I met Steven and the Zimmermans. Steven was raised in a "nearly" Catholic family. They didn't subscribe to my over-zealous ban on alcohol. Football was a family tradition in both of our houses. It was just celebrated differently in Steven's.

The first time I actually met Steven's family was football Sunday. It was a very regular occurrence for his family to gather at his mother's house and watch the Minnesota Vikings play football. They have a unique tradition of toast touchdowns. These toasts included everyone from the oldest to the youngest. While the minor children toasted with cranberry juice, they did so with their special shot glasses. My first impression of this celebration was shock and awe. It took a while for me to realize this behavior wasn't criminal. It's not an activity that we adopted in our house, but I've learned to honor it as a tradition at my in-laws.

What are some of your family's traditions related to holidays that your spouse needs to be aware of?

Him:

_____

_____

_____

_____

_____

_____

_____

_____

_____

Her:

_____

_____

_____

_____

_____

_____

_____

_____

_____

Together: If there are conflicts in these traditions, what are the plans you can develop to help make things fair for both families and help alleviate some potential conflict in the future?

_____

_____

_____

_____

_____

_____

_____

_____

_____

_____

_____

_____

_____

_____

_____

_____

_____

_____

_____

_____

_____

_____

As a couple, it is vital that you make decisions regarding your plans for serving God. You must decide where to attend church and how you will be involved in serving at your church. This is a decision that must be made by the two of you only. It will though, have the potential to affect both families in a very big way. It is important that this decision be discussed and agreed on prior to presenting it to your individual families.

For some, this may bring with it more pressure than for others. If your families both have the same religious beliefs this will be simpler than if they have very different beliefs. The sanctity of this decision is like the sanctity of the marriage, it is for the bride and groom alone.

While our family is a great voice of counsel, it is not the replacement for the voice of God through the leading of the Holy Spirit to provide the direction for your place of worship and service. Your decision should be presented to the family respectfully. You should not let your decision on how and where to serve God be unduly influenced by your families.

What are some religious traditions/beliefs that your spouse needs to be aware of?

Him:

_____

_____

_____

_____

_____

_____

_____

_____

_____

Her:

_____

_____

_____

_____

_____

_____

_____

_____

_____

If there are conflicts in these traditions, what are the plans you can develop to help make things fair for both families and help alleviate some potential conflict in the future?

Together:

_____

_____

_____

_____

_____

_____

_____

_____

_____

_____

_____

_____

_____

_____

_____

_____

_____

_____

Holiday traditions, too, can be a source of great conflict. Many families have very specific traditions that they want to continue. By discussing and developing a plan for these traditions prior to the wedding, you will find that there may be ways to accommodate both families. It is important to remember when you are discussing family traditions, that each family may have very strong emotional ties to their tradition. It is important to avoid using phrases such as "my family always" or "my family never," as this may promote defensiveness and close the door to compromise. When looking at this idea it is important to honor the traditions of both families, but leave enough flexibility to establish traditions of your own.

What are the most important family holiday traditions that your family has?

Him:

_____

_____

_____

_____

_____

_____

_____

_____

Her:

_____

_____

_____

_____

_____

_____

_____

_____

_____

What are ways that you can observe some of each family's traditions? What are family traditions that you want to bring into your family?

Together:

_____

_____

_____

_____

_____

_____

_____

_____

Family baggage and history is something every couple has to deal with as their marriage begins. This is something that you both need to be aware of so that you are not always stepping on the toes of other members of your families. For instance, is one of the parents an alcoholic, is anyone in the family a vegetarian, or maybe someone in the family has a significant pet allergy?

These are all things that need to be identified and a plan developed on how to deal with them. If this can be done prior to the wedding you can start out with everyone on the same page. This goes back to being a student of your spouse's family. Take time to get past the cliff notes and get an in-depth working knowledge of the people who will be a part of your family for the rest of your life.

A particularly important area for significant discussion is when there are ex-spouses to accommodate. If you are blending a family, it is very important that you establish parameters for dealing with the other biological parents of your children. Taking into consideration the feelings of children and honoring their parent's role in family traditions in the same way you would wish to be honored will promote harmony and unity even in the most difficult of family situations.

What, if any, unique family characteristics should your spouse be aware of?

Him:

_____

_____

_____

_____

_____

_____

_____

_____

_____

Her:

_____

_____

_____

_____

_____

_____

_____

What are ways that you can respect these unique family characteristics?

Together:

_____

_____

_____

_____

_____

_____

_____

_____

_____

_____

_____

_____

_____

_____

_____

_____

_____

_____

_____

Having Children

Deciding whether or not to have children is another critical decision. If you have a child, it's a choice that can't be unmade. Having agreement on this topic prior to the wedding is of paramount importance. While the timing of when to have children cannot always be planned, by discussing the desire to have or not to have children prior to the wedding you set yourselves up for success.

Having children will change the path of your lives forever and alter the definition of family. This single event will change the dynamics of your relationship more than any other event. It can bring with it incredible amounts of joy but can also be accompanied by an incredible amount of stress.

While you can never fully grasp how the addition of children will impact your lives, by allowing for significant discussion prior to the marriage you can move into agreement on many things concerning family.

What is your view on having children? What size of family do you feel is right for you?

Him:

_____

_____

_____

_____

_____

_____

_____

_____

Her:

_____

_____

_____

_____

_____

_____

_____

_____

_____

Children are indeed a blessing from the Lord. Psalm 127:3-4 *"Behold children are a heritage from the Lord. The fruit of the womb a reward like arrows in the hand of a warrior are the children of one's youth. Blessed is the man who fills his quiver with them."*

Children, while they will impact the relationship between a husband and wife, should never come before your relationship with your spouse. God created the husband and wife to be equals. This is not true for children. By maintaining your relationship with your spouse as the first and most important relationship, you will not only be protecting your marriage, but you will also be setting a wonderful example for your children. The most important thing you can do for your children is to love your spouse openly and honestly in front of them. This creates a home where children feel safe and secure. The importance of modeling a Biblical marriage has generational significance in that it gives your children an advantage as they move into their own marriage relationship because your children have seen a Godly marriage in their own home.

One of the great ways to protect your marriage and maintain your relationship's priority is the establishment of date night. Creating a time for romance to thrive and for you to focus your attention on your spouse, reveals their value in the relationship. Establishing a date night prior to having children and making that night non-negotiable, you will ensure that your spouse remains a top priority in your life.

What plans do you have for establishing a "Date Night?" How will you distribute the task of who plans the date?

Him:

_____

_____

_____

_____

_____

_____

_____

_____

_____

_____

_____

_____

_____

_____

Her:

_____

_____

_____

_____

_____

_____

_____

_____

_____

_____

_____

If you come into the marriage with children, it becomes crucial that you discuss the blending of your families. You must have a significant discussion on ways that you will maintain your spouse as the first and primary relationship, after God, in your life. All children must become OUR children. Therefore, it is important to discuss such topics as discipline, chores, curfews, church attendance, and parenting styles.

We recommend that you take a course in step-parenting and blended families prior to your wedding. This will help you see potential traps and pitfalls, allowing you to develop a plan for your family. The blending of two families can be one of the hardest tasks you can face in a marriage, but by having significant discussions and receiving training prior to the marriage, you will increase your likelihood of success tremendously. There are many good programs and counselors available. We recommend you seek out these services prior to the wedding.

Family night is a great way to help blend families. Having time together as a family will give you the opportunity to build the bonds of relationship. Family night could include such things as having dinner at the table, promoting conversation, or activities that encourage all members of the family to participate. It can be as simple as playing board games, going for a walk, or working on a project together that would benefit everyone. It all depends on your family's culture and preferences.

It is also important to remember that the blending of families is something that happens over time and often happens much slower than you would like. Many theories indicate that the blending of families can take as many as seven years to form a new family bond. This, of course, will vary depending on a number of factors, such as, ages of the children, involvement of birth parents, living arrangements of the children, and the consistency with maintaining parenting standards by both parents.

What plans will you make to ensure that Date Night is a priority? This might include, childcare, budgeting, and creativity.

Him:

_____

_____

_____

_____

_____

_____

_____

Her:

_____

_____

_____

_____

_____

_____

_____

What will you do to help develop family night and ensure that it is maintained as a priority? When developing your family night, keep in mind that you need to weigh the interests of your children. A high buy in rate from your children will generally result in high success rate.

Him:

_____

_____

_____

_____

_____

_____

_____

Her:

_____

_____

_____

_____

_____

_____

_____

Affair Proofing Your Marriage

We have spent several chapters talking about specific areas in marriage that will promote growth. While these are all great concepts, there is one thing that can undo all of your efforts. That is an affair.

Affairs are tragic. They can destroy years of trust, steal intimacy, and derail an otherwise healthy sex life. They can undermine finances and break apart families. Affairs are the devil's all-purpose marriage wrecker.

We want to stop affairs before they start. There are not a lot of areas in relation to sex that the Bible specific-ally prohibits, but this is one of them. It is stone tablet important. When Moses brought down the Ten Com-mandments in Exodus 20, *"Thou shalt not commit adul-tery"* was in verse 14. The danger of affairs was still present in Matthew 5:28, when Jesus says, *"But I tell you that anyone who looks at a women lustfully has already committed adultery with her in his heart."*

The truth of the matter is that the heart is where most affairs start. If that is so, then your spouse's heart becomes the paramount place of importance. You need to make it a priority to protect their heart to ensure the integrity of your marriage. It is often an emotional need or a security need that leads to extra marital relations. This is why we have to keep a close eye on our friendships with the opposite sex. Certainly, you should not restrict your friendships to your own gender. Many times having a best friend of the opposite sex, who is not your spouse, can lead to problems. There is an entire cable channel, Lifetime Movie Channel, dedicated to stories about best friends who meet the wrong person, marry them, and realize the right person was with them all along. It works great in the movies, but is rarely the case in real life.

The person you go to when you want to talk about the tough topics in life should be the person you gave your ring to. We have heard things like "I can talk to them about anything" or "they always listen to me." These should be things that can also be said of any husband or wife. If you can't talk to your spouse about things, but can talk to your friend from work, back home, or high school about it, congratulations, you have just introduced secret-keeping to your marriage.

You are marrying your spouse because you can

share anything with them and you want to share everything with them. This remains true in a healthy marriage. Remember, stay open and don't be afraid to share the good, the bad, and the ugly.

A very delicate place to watch for imbalance to sneak into friendship is when couples are good friends with other couples. It is critically important that couples have friends, even mentors, that are other couples. It prevents isolation. Adults need other adult relationships. God designed us for relationships. You need to be mindful of spending more time with your friends or the new couple in your lives, rather than with your own spouse. Double dating is great, but it doesn't replace the time when your spouse is the singular focus of your attention.

Whether date night is a fancy dinner, a walk at sunset, or movies and popcorn, it is the two hours where nothing else matters. Being with them helps quench the insecurities that invite others into your position in the relationship. If you have a best friend couple, go out with them, enjoy them, and do it as the four of you. Limit times when you are alone with the opposite sex, make it a four-way bond, not a two-way bond.

What are some ways that you can insure that Date Night will remain a critical part of your marriage?

Him:

_____

_____

_____

_____

_____

_____

_____

_____

_____

_____

_____

Her:

_____

_____

_____

_____

_____

_____

_____

_____

There are many ways to implement good boundaries in your marriage that neither of you will cross. Let's begin by talking about guarding your eyes. This is a particularly important boundary for guys. Because God designed men to be generally more visual than women, it is important to set up clear boundaries in this area.

As with everything else, the Bible lays out a clear example of the destructive power of not guarding your eyes. 2 Samuel 11:1-5 details one of the most famous elicit romances of all time. David and Bathsheba. It is a story about letting your eyes wonder. The problem is that where the eyes wondered, the man followed.

1 In the spring, when kings go forth to battle, David sent Joab with his servants and all Israel, and they ravaged the Ammonites [country] and besieged Rabbah. But David remained in Jerusalem. 2 One evening David arose from his couch and was walking on the roof of the king's house, when from there he saw a woman bathing; and she was very lovely to behold. 3 David sent and inquired about the woman. One said, Is not this Bathsheba, the daughter of Eliam and the wife of Uriah the Hittite? 4 And David sent messengers and took her. And she came in to him, and he lay with her – for she was purified from her uncleanness. Then she returned to her house. 5 And the woman became pregnant and sent and told David, I am with child. 2 Samuel 11:1-5

(AMP)

Not only did David not guard his eyes, he let them gaze upon something that they were never intended to see. He also chose to focus on what his eyes saw. Because David did not guard his eyes he followed them, and that led him to a place of sin that was destructive to himself, his family, and Bathsheba's family. This is a place where daily vigilance must be in place. You must learn to divert your eyes quickly when you run across something that can produce unwanted consequences in your life. Being quick to do this will be helpful. Having someone whom you can discuss this openly with will also help. This is a great place for you to have an accountability partner who will challenge you to remain faithful to your spouse with your eyes.

We also have the choice to focus on what we see. When we allow ourselves time to focus on what we see, we allow that thing to take root in us. It is important to follow the example laid out for us in the book of Job. The Bible says that Job made a covenant with his eyes to not look lustfully upon a girl. This is a decision that you can make with yourself and with your spouse.

1 I dictated a covenant (an agreement) to my eyes; how then could I look [lustfully] upon a girl? 2 For what portion should I have from God above [if I were lewd], and what heritage from the Almighty on high? 3 Does not calamity [justly] befall the unrighteous, and disaster the workers of iniquity? 4 Does not [God] see my ways and count all my steps? Job 31:1-5 (AMP)

While your spouse may never know if you chose to not guard your eyes, you can never fool God. Be proactive from the start. Make a covenant with your eyes. Guard your eyes and avoid the disaster that wondering eyes can bring.

What strategies will you have in place at all times that will provide a protection in the area of visual temptation?

Him:

_____

_____

_____

_____

_____

_____

_____

Her:

_____

_____

_____

_____

_____

_____

_____

_____

_____

_____

_____

_____

Spending a great deal of time alone is another area that has great potential to lead to problems. There are many reasons why one spouse might find himself or herself spending a greater amount of time alone. From jobs, family illness, or traveling, as well as many other reasons, are times a spouse may find themselves having a significant time alone. When this time is used constructively it provides a great opportunity to build your relationship with God or often even provides time for much needed rest.

However, it also provides the opportunity for problems to exacerbate in your marriage. Often loneliness can be a by-product of prolonged times of separation. This can be something that drives one spouse to seek out ways to eliminate loneliness that can become danger zones. There are also ways to make sure that these danger zones are avoided.

One way is by having frequent contact with your spouse during the periods of separation. Utilizing text messaging, phone calls, face time, and emails is a great way to keep in contact, even if one of you is on the other side of the world. Involvement in church activities will provide a productive outlet to decrease loneliness. Involvement with friends of the same sex is yet another way to alleviate the negative effects of loneliness. Discussion of these ideas and planning prior to encountering these times is vital. Having a specific plan in place will help ensure that your marriage thrives.

What are some safeguards that you can put in place to help with extended periods of separation from your spouse?

Him:

_____

_____

_____

_____

_____

_____

_____

_____

Her:

_____

_____

_____

_____

_____

_____

_____

_____

Physical contact in a way that promotes intimacy is a line that defines whether an emotional affair has made a transition to a full-blown affair. The common defense is "we are just friends." Do friends hold hands? How long do friends hug? How often do friends kiss? Do friends ever kiss on the lips?

These may seem like obvious boundaries that are common sense, however, every act of adultery is a series of choices to go beyond a boundary. It is important to talk about boundaries. Putting those boundaries in place from the beginning will ensure that obvious decisions are not left to be made in a moment of weakness. The following are boundaries that have been proven to be helpful to many couples:

- Never ride alone in a car with a person of the opposite sex that is not a blood family member.

- Never meet with a person of the opposite sex alone in a private place or with doors closed.

- Always allow your spouse access to the passwords of all email/Facebook/Twitter accounts. Allow your spouse full access to your phone at any time.

- Always maintain a relationship with a person to

whom you give permission, to ask any questions about your behavior, relationship with God, and with your spouse.

- Never share emotional issues with any person of the opposite sex that you haven't previously shared with your spouse.

- Make sure all casual texting is done for informational purposes only, and that your spouse has access to them all times.

What other boundaries will you put in place for your marriage?

Him:

_____

_____

_____

_____

_____

_____

_____

_____

_____

Her:

_____

_____

_____

_____

_____

_____

_____

_____

_____

_____

_____

Finally, we want to end with the concept that if the grass seems greener on the other side of the fence, then you haven't been doing a good job watering your own grass. By making sure that you are diligent to treat your marriage as the second most valuable relationship in your life, right behind God, and spending time every day enriching your relationship with your spouse, you will ensure a healthy, happy, and long lasting marriage.

A concept that has served us well is "whatever you focus on grows." Stay focused on God and your spouse and watch your marriage grow into something amazing.

Melisa was born and raised in Western Oklahoma. She grew up in the Baptist Church and moved quickly into entrepreneurship as the owner of a floral shop and style shop. This was interrupted by a twenty-year journey into a marriage that was not God's best for her. It did produce three great kids, Mark, Levon, and Mariah, all of whom are serving God today. Melisa worked for the Oklahoma University College of Nursing for nine years before moving on to a staff position at Victory Church and rising to be the Small Groups Director; a position she has held for the last two years.

Steve was born and raised in Minnesota. He was raised nearly Catholic, and after firing God, re-emerged as a Presbyterian. Steve brings twenty years of all types of relationship chaos history into their marriage of nine years. Steve is a committed teacher, small group leader, and prayer partner. He has displayed the same devotion to the bride of Christ as he has to his bride, Melisa.

Together, Steve and Melisa have purposed to bring all their experiences and training to bear in preparing couples for marriage, enriching marriages, and repairing marriages. They have a special place in their hearts for speaking into blended families as they have walked that path since they met. Their mission continues to be "Building and Rebuilding Bridges in Relationships".

CPSIA information can be obtained
at www.ICGtesting.com
Printed in the USA
FFOW02n1435010415
12302FF